The **SIMPLY** wo

craft book

Lois Rock

A LION BOOK

Oxford · Batavia · Sydney

Published by
Lion Publishing Corporation
1705 Hubbard Avenue, Batavia, Illinois, 60510, USA
ISBN 0 7459 2503 0

First edition 1993

Acknowledgments
Studio photography by John Williams Studios, Thame
Illustrations by Helen Herbert
Additional photographs: Ardea (Joan Beames) 13;
Lion Publishing 7 (top); Oxford Scientific Films
(Scott Camazine) 4, (Owen Newman) 5, (G. I. Bernard) 6,
(Hans Reinhard) 8, (Rodger Jackman) 11;
Willi Rauch 7 (lower)

Library of Congress CIP Data applied for

Printed and bound in Malaysia.

Many thanks to all the craft-workers who snipped, stitched, sawed, glued and painted to make sure that all the projects gave simply wonderful results: Anna Mayhew, Daniel Rock, Davina Rock, Sebastian Rock, Henry Tickler.

Thanks also to those who modeled the clothes: Laura Church, Marc Church, Sebastian Rock.

Younger children may need grown-up supervision when doing some of the projects in this book.

BRILLIANT IDEAS...
from an amazing world

Have you ever looked at the wonderful designs in the world around you and thought: Wow! that's brilliant—I wish I could make something like that!

Have you ever looked at your collection of treasures—shells and stones, scraps of fabric, special types of paper, bits and pieces of wood—and thought: There must be something I could do with those, something to show how beautiful they are, something *worthwhile!*

Have you ever looked at the heaps of trash that people throw out—old newspapers, boxes, clothes—and been sad to see how much is being wasted? Surely some of it could be used again?

Or have you ever looked at something you have made all by yourself and felt a glow of satisfaction because you know that you've really achieved something? Even if you think that what you've made is not quite perfect, you still know that it's a personal best, and you still feel good about it.

Next time, perhaps, what you make will be even better.

This book is about all those things. It's about enjoying the world around us and finding ideas for what to make from what you see.

It's about deciding how to use materials, new and old, in the best way possible, to get real value out of them. That means making the most of the way they look and the way they feel, and turning them into something useful or something that really brightens up the world.

It's about discovering your own talents and just how clever you are at designing things and making them.

At the same time, it shows you how to be careful with

CONTENTS

the world's resources, so that none are wasted, so that the environment is not polluted, and so that you don't greedily snatch for yourself resources that could better be shared with other people.

And this book is about sharing, too. Some of the craft ideas show you how to make things to give as gifts. Others help you save money, so that you and your family can think about sharing what you save with other people around the world who need that kind of help.

Today, many people are concerned about using the world's resources in ways that are right for the Earth and fair for the people who live in it. In many ways it just seems like good sense. However, the people who put this book together did so for a special reason: we all believe that the world was made by God, and that the amazing designs in the world around us are his work, his creation. We believe that he made

us the way we are and has given us our ability to design and create things. We believe that he wanted us to find brilliant ideas in his amazing world so we could use its resources in right ways: wisely, carefully, and for the good of all. This book is to provide ideas that will help us keep to his plan!

Get Busy!

Get busy right away organizing your craft corner. That way, you'll be able to stay on top of your projects, and not end up in a total mess.

Look how the birds get organized in spring, collecting what they need from far and wide. Even materials that seem unpromising can be used in a clever way—just use your imagination!

CARDBOARD CITY

Put unwanted cardboard boxes to good use by turning them into the furniture for your craft room.

Sometimes it will be best to use the boxes just as they are. Other times, you may want to decorate them.

★ Table
Find four tall boxes all the same size to make legs for your table. Cut a tray shape from an even larger box to make a cardboard top. Now you have a disposable table that is just great for crafts using paint and glue.

★ Bin
Almost any box makes a good bin. Collect same-size boxes that line up in a neat row to store your craft materials in. Find a large one for a trash can.

★ File
Cut sturdy narrow boxes like this to make a file for papers and magazines.

Living with cardboard may be fun for you, but it's no joke in some parts of the world, where many people have to make their homes from cardboard boxes. If you can save money by reusing cardboard, it's worth thinking of ways to give that money to help people who need it.

OVERALL SUCCESS

Protect your clothes from paint and glue with an apron you make yourself.

scissors

pencil and newspaper

needle

pins

heavy cotton fabric, about 24in. x 32in.

sewing thread to match

bright thread to contrast

7ft. x 1in. cotton braid

1 Ask a friend to hold a piece of newspaper up against you and mark out the shape of an apron on it.

2 Fold the paper down the center longways. Use a ruler to make all the sketched lines straight and the bottom corners square. Cut out this shape through the folded paper.

3 Check the pattern against you and adjust it if you need to.

4 Lay the pattern on your fabric, with the center fold running down along a single thread in the weave. Draw a line $1/2$ in. outside the pattern. Cut out the fabric apron on this outer line.

5 Fold in the edges $1/2$ in. in this order: first the two slant edges, then the top; next fold up the bottom edge, and finally fold in the straight sides. (This will keep all the corners neat.) Pin the folds in place.

6 Now stitch the edge in place with matching thread. Use a small, neat in-and-out stitch, keeping the stitches about $1/4$ in. from the folded edge, or a herringbone stitch.

7 Pin one end of the braid to a top corner, allowing about 1in. extra. Hold the apron against you and measure how long the neck strap needs to be. Pin the other end, again allowing 1in. extra, and snip off the braid.

8 Cut the remaining braid in half and pin one end to each of the sides with 1in. extra. Stitch all the braid in

place with a pattern of dot and straight stitches in decorative thread. (This uses up the 1in. extra you allowed.)

★ Cut a pocket the size and shape you want from spare fabric.
  First stitch the top edge down.
  Then hem it in place on the other three sides like a patch (see page 9).
  Sew a square of dots at each top corner for extra strength.

2
Bright Ideas

The world is full of bright colors and the most amazing patterns. Here's everything you need to help you come up with beautiful designs of your own!

SIMPLE STENCILING

The simplest stencils are made by cutting a paper snowflake: you just fold the paper and cut holes along the folded edges with scissors. Unfold the paper for a brilliant stencil!

If you are able to use a craft knife, you can cut a wider range of patterns.

safety craft knife and cutting mat

pencil and paper

stencil card

stencil brushes

paper to stencil on

thick paint, either poster paints or acrylic

Be sure to select a safety craft knife.

1 Copy the designs for stencil patterns shown here onto paper. Pencil in the parts where the paint shows. These are the parts that need to be cut in the stencil.

2 Now transfer the design onto the stencil card. Put the paper design on the card and press heavily with a pencil to mark the outline of the colored shapes on the card. Lift off the paper.

3 Put the card on the cutting mat and cut out the shapes with a craft knife.

4 To stencil on paper: lay the paper out on a flat surface. Put a tiny piece of sticky putty in each corner of the stencil to hold it in place while you work, and press it down on the paper.

5 Dip the stencil brush in the paint so just the tip is covered. Dab twice on a piece of scrap paper to get rid of extra paint, then dab lightly through the holes in your stencil.

6 Repeat the pattern as often as you like.

★ Use a different brush for each different color.

★ Notice how a stencil works, with bridges of card holding the design together. Work out your own designs that follow this rule.

Noteworthy

Whenever you use paper, think of the trees from which it is made. If you look at a tree trunk or branch that has been sawn through, you can see a pattern of rings. Each one represents one year of growth.

Think how long it takes for trees to grow.

Think of the real value of a piece of paper that has been made from them.

Here are some good ways to make use of scraps of paper that might otherwise be thrown away. This is recycling at its simplest.

TRUFFLES

4 oz. chocolate chips
3 tbsp. whipping cream
¼ tsp. cinnamon
2 oz. ground almonds
chocolate vermicelli

Heat the whipping cream in a small pan until it is nearly boiling.

Lift the pan onto a heatproof surface.

Stir in the chocolate chips until they are melted.
Stir in the cinnamon and ground almonds.
Pour the mixture into a shallow pan and leave in the refrigerator to cool and go firm.

Pour some vermicelli onto a plate. Roll a teaspoonful of the mix in the vermicelli. When coated, roll it into a ball.

Make more truffles in the same way.

GO BY THE BOOK

Beautiful notebooks have so many uses: for the addresses and phone numbers of your friends, for keeping a diary of important events, for lists and plans, for bright ideas of all the things you'd like to make...

cutting board and safety craft knife or scissors

needle

ruler and pencil
clean scrap paper

thin card

decorated paper

thread

glue

Be sure to select a safety craft knife.

1 Cut your scrap paper into pages, the size you want the book to be when it is laid open. You can make a successful book with 5–8 sheets.

2 Make the sheets into a neat pile and fold them in half where the book will hinge. Press.

3 Thread the needle. Make a big stitch as shown, and tie the ends into a knot on the outside so the stitch holds the pages together. Make one or two more stitches in the same way along the fold of the book.

4 Cut a piece of card, a little larger all around than the pages. On the outside, mark the center line where it will fold and lay a ruler on it. Draw a heavy line with a pencil. Then check that it will fold easily.

5 Cut a piece of decorated paper 1in. wider all around than the card. Center the card on the paper. Fold the paper in along the top and bottom edges and crease. Then fold each corner in a triangle before turning in the side edges. Lift the

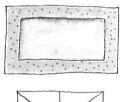
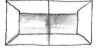

paper so you can spread glue underneath the turned down part, then press into place.

6 Check that the pages fit neatly inside the decorated cover and trim if necessary. Then spread glue over the front and back pages and stick them to the inside cover of the book.

★ Use decorated paper for the bottom page of your booklet. That way, the stuck-down ends will look extra good too.

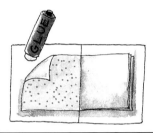

LOG BOOK

The wood back for this notepad gives you something to press on when you write, and reminds you of the beauty in the trees that people use to make paper.

handsaw and cutting table

hand drill

sandpaper

pencil

scissors

thick needle

scrap piece of log or wood

yarn

clean scrap paper

Check with a grown-up before using woodworking tools. Follow the instructions for where and how to use them exactly.

1 Think what would be the best size for your log book. Cut a piece of wood or a slice of log that is a little larger than this all around.

2 Sand the wood smooth (avoid the bark if you are using a log).

3 Cut your paper into roughly even size pieces to fit on the block.

4 Work out the best place for two holes to fasten the paper onto the wood. Mark these with a cross.

5 Ask a grown-up to help you find a place to use the drill. Select a drill bit to make a hole about 1/4 in. wide. Drill two holes as marked.

6 Thread the needle with the yarn and stitch your pile of paper to the block (the needle will go through only a few sheets at a time).

7 Tie the yarn into a bow and trim.

Box Office Success

Here are ideas for making all kinds of boxes. They're great for storing precious items, or for packaging gifts.

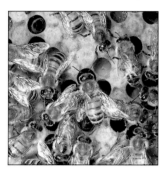

Bees must be some of the most avid storers in the natural world. They build honeycombs, six-sided 'jars' made of wax. Each is filled with honey and a lid put on, to keep it safe for when they need it.

BOX BASICS

Everyone needs to know how to make a basic box with a lid. It's fun to practice until you have the knack.

cutting board and safety craft knife, or scissors

ruler

pencil

thin card

glue (or double-sided tape)

tape

1 Organize yourself with a piece of card large enough for the box itself. Decide on the size of the base of the box. Draw a rectangle this size in the center of your card.

2 Decide on the height of the box and draw a rectangle around the base this far away on every side. Now draw another rectangle around this, $1/2$ inch away. Cut out this shape.

3 Mark cutting lines from the edge to the line of the base. Snip,

4 Fold the edges along the lines of the base, as shown.

5 Unfold the edges and cut the corners as shown.

6 Fold in $1/2$ in. along the side edges. Unfold.

7 Now fold the box up and glue the flaps to hold the corners square. Tape the inside for extra strength if you wish.

8 Spread glue on the underside of the $1/2$ in. edge and fold this in neatly.

★ Make a lid in the same way, but make the base of the lid $1/8$ in. bigger all around than the base of

the box (this measurement
will vary depending on
the thickness of the card
you use).

★ Make boxes-to-fit-in-
boxes to create loads of
compartments for small
items.

★ Try using your skill at
box making to make a box
with a triangular base.
Then try any shape with
straight sides you can
think of.

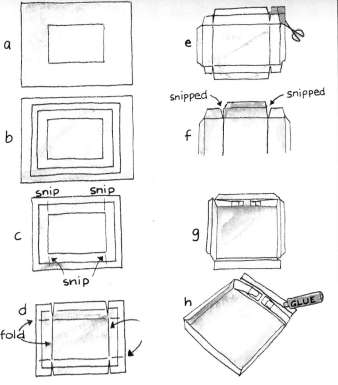

a

b

c

snip   snip

d
fold

e

snipped   snipped
f

g

h   GLUE

TOP
DRAWER

Make a sliding top for
a shallow box. Fold a
piece of card to the size
of your box as shown
and tape or glue it
together. Slide it
carefully into place.

★ How do you think
you could adapt this
idea to make a set of
cardboard drawers?

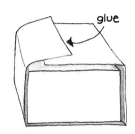

glue

Package Deals

Explore the natural world to discover the many designs for packages for precious things. Look at buds for flowers and leaves, seedpods for seeds, nests for eggs... and many, many more.

They'll provide you with loads of inspiration for your own ideas.

BAGS OF FUN

scissors
pencil and paper
ruler
needle
pins

cotton fabric
thread
cord

1 Draw the size of bag you want to make as a rectangle on the paper. Add about 1in. to the top. Now add another $1/2$ in. all around. This is your pattern. Cut it out.

2 Fold your fabric along a line of thread in the weave and lay the pattern on top with the straight edge along the fold. Cut out the fabric double, and slit through the fold.

3 Put the fabric right sides together and stitch with a neat, small backstitch. Start and end 1in. from the top edge of each side and stitch $1/2$ in. in from the side and bottom edges. Turn the bag right sides out.

4 Fold in the unsewn side edges $1/2$ in. and then neatly fold in the top edges. Stitch all the way around the top and open sides with a small, neat in-and-out stitch, about $1/4$ in. from the folded edge.

5 Turn the top edge in to the point where the sides join. Pin in place.

6 Now stitch one row of neat in-and-out stitches through all thicknesses to make a channel for the cord. Sew the beginning and end very firmly with a few over-and-over stitches, or a dot stitch.

7 Cut two pieces of cord, each at least three times the width of the top of the pattern.

8 Hook a safety pin through one end of a piece of cord and close it. Use the pin to push the cord through the channel you stitched in the top. Knot the ends together.

9 Repeat with the other cord, but start at the opposite end so the knot is made on the other side.

★ If you wish, stitch a pattern on the side of the bag before you sew it.

★ Make your own cord by braiding yarn together. Knot the ends into a tassel.

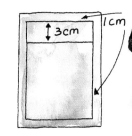

3cm   1cm

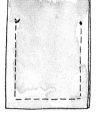

GET WEAVING

round plastic tub or cardboard tube

scissors

needle

tape

yarn

1 The basket will be as wide as your tub or tube, and a little shorter. Choose the size you want, then carefully snip the top edge into notches about 1/4 in. apart. Check that you have an odd number.

2 Tape one end of yarn inside the top of the tube. Now wind it down through a notch, outside the tub or tube, across the bottom and back up into the notch directly opposite the first. Continue across the top and into the next notch to the right, then back up into the notch directly opposite.

3 Continue winding round and round in this way until the loom is full. You will be left with the yarn at the bottom.

4 Unwind another yard of this yarn and snip it. Thread the needle and begin to weave around the outer edge of the base. Go over one thread, under the next, and so on. Every time you do a round, pull it tightly towards the center.

5 Keep weaving until the base is covered with weaving and then up the side. When you need more yarn simply leave about 2in. of the old bit tucked inside and start a new piece, again leaving about 2in.

6 Add as many different colors as you wish to make stripes.

7 When you are 1in. from the top of the tube, stop weaving. Snip the thread across the top of the tube and tie them off in pairs, using an overhand knot. Tie in the weaving thread with one pair. When you get to the last three threads, tie those together.

8 Trim the loose ends if you wish, but always leave at least 3/4 in. so the knots don't untie.

9 Knot the ends where you joined the yarn inside the basket.

★ Can you work out how you could make a lid for baskets like these?

This bird's nest is a bit like a basket woven from twigs and grass.

Creature Comforts

Think of furry animals snuggling down in their winter-time den... think of birds lying snug in a feathered nest... think of cuddling down among cushions, of lying warm and cozy in a soft bed...

Birds and beasts spend hours collecting soft things to line their den. Collect scraps and use your craft skills to make your own den extra cozy.

LOG CABIN

This simple patchwork grows out from the center, with the pieces overlapping like the timber in a log cabin.

ruler

scissors

needle

scraps of cotton fabric

thread

larger piece of cotton fabric for the cushion back

cushion pad

1 Collect scraps of cotton fabric and tear them into strips all the same width—say, 2in.

2 Take one strip, and cut off a square piece for the center.

3 Take another piece and cut off a same-size square. Place the right sides together and sew a line of small neat back stitches 1/2 in. from the edge.

4 Now turn the piece and add a strip as shown. Cut off the piece that overlaps.

5 Keep turning and adding strips as shown. Your patchwork will grow and grow.

6 When it is a little larger than your cushion pad, cut a plain piece of fabric the same size.

7 Sew the patchwork and the plain piece around three and a half sides, right sides together, 1/2 in. in from the edge.

8 Turn the cushion cover right side out, carefully insert the pad. Fold the 1/2 in. inside and stitch the opening closed with an over-and-over stitch.

★ Think about the colors you use. Try building squares of the same color.

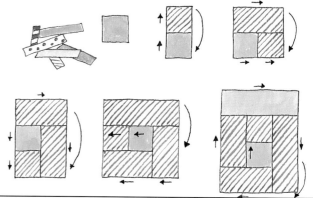

AND SEW TO BED

Making a quilt is a wonderful way to make use of old clothes, and to build up a treasure trove of memories.

Woven cotton fabric is easy to use. It's best to stick with one sort of fabric for a quilt that will last and last.

scissors

needle

card square, 4in. x 4in.

endless scraps of fabric

thread

old blanket or polyester batting

old sheet of plain cotton fabric

thicker yarn

1 Begin by collecting squares of fabric, all cut 4in. x 4in. Always cut the squares so a straight edge of the pattern lines up with a line of thread in the weave. Store the squares in bundles of 4 or 5 alike.

2 When you have enough, choose a bundle of 4 and a bundle of 5 that go together and arrange them in a checker pattern.

3 Sew them into three strips, using a small neat backstitch, and press the seam flat. Then sew the three strips together, trying to match the corners as nearly as possible.

4 When you have made enough big squares for a bedspread, decide how you want to arrange them. Then you sew the big squares into long strips, and the long strips together. (It will help if you can use a sewing machine for this.)

5 To finish the quilt: lay the patchwork on top of the old blanket or batting. Trim to the same size.

6 Lay the sheet or cotton fabric on top of the patchwork. Trim to the same size.

7 Stitch all three layers together using large in-and-out stitches. Then use a sewing machine to sew around three and three-quarter edges.

8 Turn the quilt out so the patchwork is on top. Sew the opening closed with tiny over-and-over stitches.

9 Lay the quilt flat. Pinch all three layers together at the corner of each nine-patch square. Thread a needle with yarn and take a stitch from the bottom through all three layers, then back down about $1/4$ in. away. Tie the ends together and trim the ends. Repeat for the corners of all the big squares. (You can add more tufts if you wish, for a fluffy look.)

★ If a quilt seems too large a job for you, try making the squares into cushion covers, or a small blanket for the car or beach.

★ Try making a quilt like this as a project in your school or community. If everyone makes just two or three squares, you can quickly get a quilt together . . . for yourselves, or to give away.

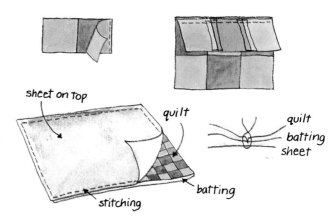

sheet on top

quilt

quilt
batting
sheet

stitching

batting

All Sewn Up

The best clothes are ones that are right for the occasion... and right for the kind of person you are.

The style of this T-shirt is comfortable and practical for warm summer days when you want to have fun.

Just look at the glorious colors and patterns of the world around you! You'll find them hard to equal, but they'll give you wonderful ideas for your own clothes.

TERRIFIC T

Ask a friend to help measure you when you start this project.

measuring tape
pencil and paper
large scissors
pins
needle
ruler
scrap paper

fabric, about 3ft x 5ft
sewing thread to match
bright thread to contrast
about 4in. thin ribbon or cord
2 medium-sized buttons

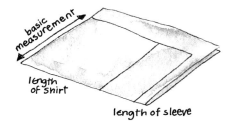

1 First, fold your fabric in half lengthwise and lay it out on the table. Make sure the fold runs along a single thread in the weave. Slit the fabric carefully along the fold.

2 Now work out how big to cut the pieces. Flex your arm muscles, and ask a friend to measure across from the fattest part of one muscle to the other, and add 1in. more. This is your Basic Measurement. Measure this distance across the fabric from the slit edge, and draw a line parallel to the slit all the way down the fabric. Cut the remaining fabric away through both thicknesses.

3 Now ask your friend to measure you from the highest point of your shoulder to a little bit longer than you want the T-shirt to be. Mark the length on the fabric and cut out. These two pieces are the back and front.

4 Measure from your shoulder to your elbow. Halve the result, and add 1in. Mark the length on the fabric and cut out. These two pieces are the sleeves.

5 Fold the front piece in half and cut out a scoop 2in. deep at the center, tapering to nothing 5in. in from the shoulders.

6 Turn the scoop under $1/2$ in. and stitch in place with an in-and-out stitch $1/4$ in. from the fold.

7 Sew the shoulders together 5in. on one side and $2^{1}/_{2}$ in. on the other, using matching thread and a backstitch. Keep your lines of stitching $1/2$ in. from the edge.

8 Turn in $1/2$ in. along the back edge of the neck and the open part of the shoulder. Stitch down with an in-and-out stitch.

9 Center the sleeves on the shoulder and pin in place. Backstitch, starting and ending $1/2$ in. from the short edge of each sleeve.

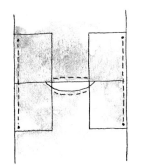

10 Stitch the sleeve seams and side seams, using a backstitch.

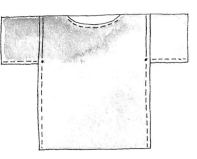

11 Turn up the bottom edge $1/2$ in. and then turn it over again. Sew it in place, remembering to press the seam open at each side. Turn up the bottom edges of the sleeves in the same way.

12 Use matching thread to sew a button on the open side of the front at the place where the neck scoop begins. (See page 9.)

13 Fold the cord or ribbon in half to make a button loop. Use matching thread to stitch this in place on the back edge of the neck. It should match up with the button, and be just large enough to slip over it easily.

Knit Wit

Notice how birds and animals keep themselves warm in winter: some animals grow a thick winter coat; birds fluff up their feathers to trap an extra layer of warm air around them.

The wool that keeps sheep warm can be used to keep people warm, too.

Look in the back of the book for instructions on how to knit and then make these winter warmers.

GET AHEAD

knitting needles, size 5
thick, blunt-ended needle
scissors

medium thick yarn, in 2 or 3 colors

Ask a grown-up who knows about knitting to help you get the right thickness of yarn for the needles.

1 Cast on 12 stitches.

2 Knit until you have a strip that will fit around your head if you stretch it just a bit. Cast off.

3 Thread the cut ends on a needle and stitch the strip into a circle. An over-and-over stitch that catches the edge will work well.

4 Make a pompom: first thread the needle with about 12in. of thread and put to one side.

5 Wind more yarn around two fingers, up and down the length, for about 80 turns. Snip the end.

6 Use the needle and thread to wrap two loops around the yarn on your fingers. Push the needle between your two fingers as shown, then gently ease the yarn off and tie the loop to make a tight sheaf.

7 Tie the loop tightly. Use the ends to sew the pompom to the headband. Make as many as you like to get the effect you want!

KNIT MITT

Make a very simple mitten from a square of knitting. You need the same materials as for the headband.

1 Cast on enough stitches to make a piece of knitting wide enough to cover from the base of your fingers to your wrist. Try 36.

2 Keep knitting until you have a piece long enough to wrap around your hand, stretching it slightly.

3 Cast off and join the knitting into a circle.

4 Thread the needle with a length of yarn.

5 Slip the knitting over your hand and pinch it together between your second and third fingers. Take a single stitch through the knitting to mark the place.

6 Make a pompom as described for the headband, and stitch this in place at the point you marked, to hold the two edges together.

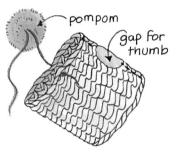

pompom

gap for thumb

7 Make another mitten in the same way.

★ You can add as many pompoms as you like to these mittens!

SUPER SCARF

You will need a lot of yarn and loads of patience to knit a scarf. You can make a good one in medium-thick yarn with 50 stitches. Keep knitting until it is the length you want!

★ Try adding stripes. Always change color on an odd-numbered row. Knot the ends together at the side edge. Leave the ends long enough for you to thread them on a needle and weave them into the knit for about 1in. so they don't show.

★ Make a fringe for the ends. Cut yarn into 6in. lengths and make a bundle of 5. Bend this in the middle. Push a crochet hook into one corner of the scarf, catch the bundle of yarn in the middle, and pull it through. Now tuck the cut ends through the loop and pull to make a snug knot.

On the Mend

It's wonderful to see how the natural world slowly but surely tries to mend any damage: think of wild plants colonizing an area of wasteland, of living creatures moving back as the habitat is restored ... It has been designed with an inbuilt recycling and renewal plan.

Mending things is a very satisfying way of using your creative talents, and at the same time using the world's resources well. You save money, too, and that can help you to be more generous to others.

BUTTON UP

Drag out all the things you shoved to the back of the closet because they were missing a button. If you ask your family and friends, you're bound to find someone with a collection of old buttons, and you can sew a new one on with no trouble!

needle
scissors
toothpick or blunt needle

button
thread

1 thread the needle and make a knot in one end. Sew down through the fabric at the point where the button should go, then come up about $1/8$ in. away.

2 Now take the needle up through one hole in the button and down through the other, then down through the fabric as before. Push the toothpick or blunt needle between the button and the fabric, to make a little space.

3 Now continue sewing up through the button and back down through the fabric 4–6 times.

4 Push the needle up just to one side of the thread. Remove the toothpick. Wind the thread around the bunch of threads 3 or 4 times.

5 Take the needle back down through the fabric and take three back stitches on top of each other to finish off.

★ Some buttons have a little stem. You don't need to prop these on a toothpick or wind the thread around.

★ Some buttons have four holes. You can stitch these in a number of ways, as shown.

★ Use colored clay that bakes hard in the oven to make your own buttons. Use a toothpick to make two holes in each before you bake them. You may need to leave a piece of toothpick in each hole while they bake, to keep the hole from closing up.

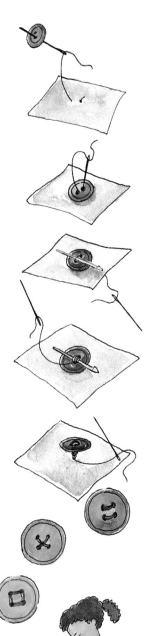

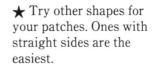

YOUR OWN LITTLE PATCH

Cut a matching patch for a mend you don't want to show. Cut a contrasting patch to decorate your clothes. Patches are great for covering stains and small holes.

★ Try other shapes for your patches. Ones with straight sides are the easiest.

★ Use fancy thread and stitching as well as strong hemming to make your patch even brighter.

scissors

needle

pins

fabric of the same type as the garment

thread

1 Cut a square patch that covers the stain or hole generously, with ¹/₂ in. extra all around.

2 Turn in the ¹/₂ in. around all the edges. Tack these in place with large stitches.

3 Now pin the patch in place. Tack it with large stitches if you think it might slip around.

4 Use a hemming stitch to attach the patch permanently. Remove the pins and any tacking.

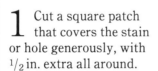
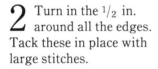

FIXIT FUN

It is very satisfying to fix things. Arm yourself with your sewing kit, plus a roll of tape, some glue, and an assortment of boxes that you have found or made. Go through your things: mending, stitching, and gathering into boxes and sorting.

★ Salvage bits and pieces that might come in handy— buttons, bits of card or paper— and store them in boxes.

★ Sort the things that you are going to throw out: can any be recycled or taken to a secondhand shop?

★ Throw out the rest. You'll feel great when it's all done!

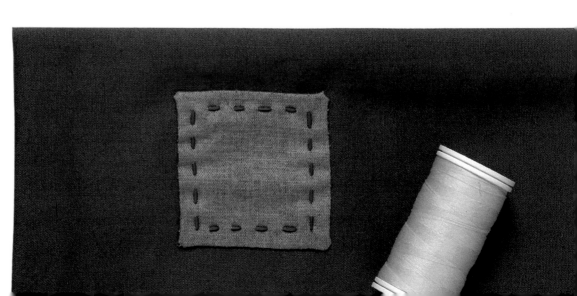

Fun and Games

The world is full of amazing things... and there you are with nothing to do.

Here are great ideas for turning everyday things into games you can enjoy making *and* playing.

Invite a friend to share the fun!

LEAF LOOKALIKES

Make your own memory game with these leaf prints. Discover the amazing variety of different leaves that there are, their different shapes and colors.

You'll need at least twenty different types to make this game a good one, and you can go on building your set to forty or even fifty.

paint pots or lids from jars

paintbrushes

scissors

newspaper

fresh leaves, as many different types as you can find, but small enough to fit on the size of card you make

poster paint (green, yellow, blue, black and red)

scrap paper

white paper, cut into squares

thin card in one plain color, cut into playing-card size squares

glue

1 Organize the place where you'll be working, with two large pads of scrap paper.

2 Mix a little paint in a shade of green to match your first leaf. You may have to add some of the other colors to get it right.

3 Take this leaf and place it underside up on one pad. Paint all over it. Now lay the leaf paint side up on the clean pad.

4 Take a square of white paper and press it carefully over the painted leaf. Rub gently over it with a finger. Then peel the leaf and paper apart, and set the paper aside for the paint to dry.

5 Repaint the leaf as before, and make some more prints, until you have two good ones that look the same.

6 Now make prints of the other leaves, mixing up different shades of green as required.

7 When the leaf prints are dry, cut out the two best of each kind and glue one print on each square card. Let the glue dry.

★ You play the memory game with 2–4 people.

Mix up the pairs of cards and lay them all face down on the table.

Taking turns, each player turns over two cards. If they turn over a pair, they take those cards away. If they don't, they turn them back over, leaving them in the same place.

Play until all the pairs have been found. The winner is the person with the most pairs.

★ Give someone else a chance to shine: see who can identify the most leaves correctly!

THREE IN A ROW

Try this variation on an old game. It's not as easy as it looks!

ruler
pencil
scissors
marker pen

stiff card
scraps of paper in different colors
glue
tape

1 Follow the instructions on page 4 to make a square, shallow box with a lid. The box should be about 5in. square.

2 Use a marker pen to draw a checked pattern on the lid.

3 Glue two other colors of paper onto scraps of card. Cut three shapes from one piece, and three different shapes from the other.

★ Each player has one set of three pieces. They lay them down, one at a time, in turn, each trying to make a row.

When all six pieces are on the board, the players then take turns to move their pieces, until one of them makes a row of three.

★ Make playing pieces from scraps of wood or modeling clay.

★ You can use all kinds of scrap materials to make this game. Try sewing fabric squares into a patchwork, and use this to make a bag (see page 5). Play with buttons.

★ For instant outdoor fun, mark a playing board with stalks and play with leaves and flowers.

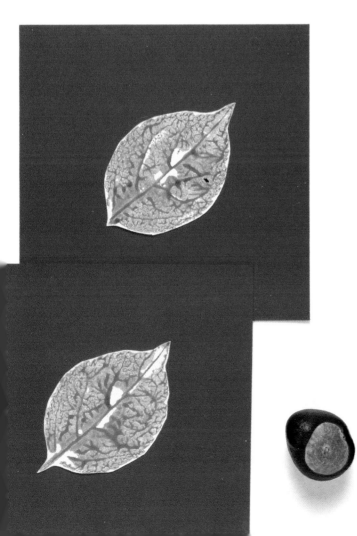

Animal Friends

For those lonely times when there's no one around, it can be nice to have an animal friend.

But it's not always possible to have a live pet... so make your own trouble-free animal friends instead.

These mice like juggling, performing, flying through the air, and snuggling into your bed. They make no noise, don't smell, and never need feeding. Their natural cousins are much happier too, because they can go on living outdoors!

MIGHTY MICE

Learn to juggle with just three mice. You feel quite brilliant when you get the knack of it, and you can keep friends and family entertained for ages with your skill.

pencil and paper

scissors

pins

needle

scraps of plain woven fabric, cotton or silk

decorative thread

matching thread

sand or rice

1 Copy the shape for a basic mouse onto plain paper. Plan your design for the face and tail. Now draw another line 1/2 in. away all around.

2 Lay this pattern on the scraps of fabric. Make sure the straight edge lines up with a single thread in the weave. Pin the pattern in place and cut around the edge.

3 Cut a matching piece for each mouse.

4 Place the two pieces on a table, right side up and noses together. Pencil the eye and ear on each.

5 Stitch the eyes with a knot stitch. Outline the ears with backstitch.

6 Take three short pieces of the decorative thread and braid them into a tail. Knot both ends.

7 Put each pair of pieces right sides together and pin the tail in the right place but inside the mouse. Stitch around, leaving the straight edge open. Turn right sides

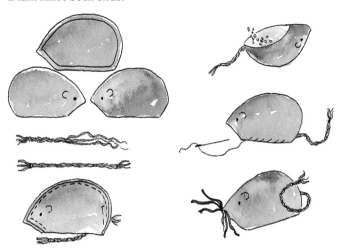

out—and the tail is now on the outside!

8 Fill each mouse about two thirds full with rice or sand. Tuck in the unsewn edges and close the opening with an over-and-over stitch.

9 Fill the needle with 5–6 strands of decorative thread and sew these through the nose. Remove the needle and tie the threads into a reef knot. Trim the thread to make whiskers.

★ If you prefer, use fabric crayons to mark the face.

★ Learn how to juggle! Practice throwing one mouse in the air and catching it. Try with each hand.

Now practice juggling with two in your best hand. As the one in the air comes down, you throw the other one up.

When you can juggle with two in either hand, try this simple juggling with three.

THREE AROUND

Here's a much simpler juggling game to play with two friends. You'll certainly find out something about working as a team!

Stand in a ring and all three throw to your right at the same time. Catch with your left.

How long can you keep throwing?

Flying Ace

How amazing to be able to fly! Think of the wonderful way that birds and insects have been designed so that they can soar and swoop, hover and glide.

   With a kite tugging in your hand, you can just begin to imagine what it might be like to fly yourself...

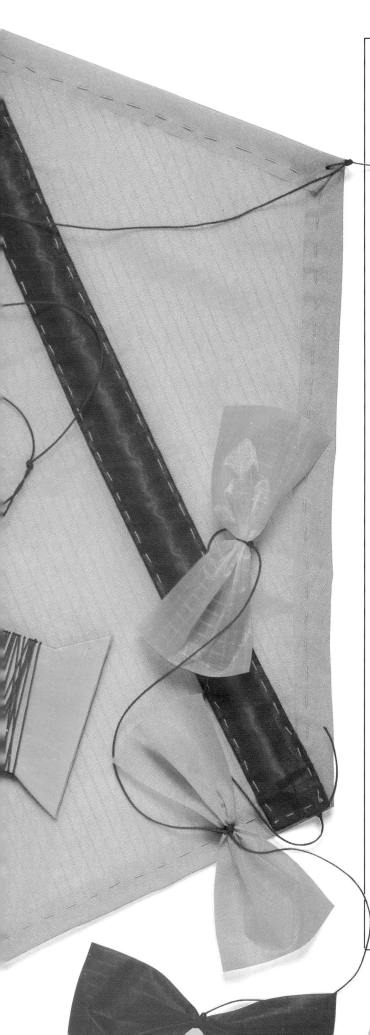

KITE

ruler

paper and pencil

scissors

needle

a piece of ripstop nylon, silk or lightweight canvas, about 16in. x 16in.

Two 1/4 in. thick wooden dowels, each about 10in. long

strong sewing thread

thin, strong yarn

colored scraps of fabric

kite twine or thin, strong string

Safety first! Never fly your kite where it might get tangled in overhead wires. Never fly a kite when a thunderstorm threatens.

1 Copy the shape shown here onto paper. Add 1/2 in. all around, to turn in.

2 Lay the pattern on the fabric, with the top edge running along a single thread in the weave. Draw around the pattern. Cut out. Draw two straight pencil lines where the sticks go.

3 Turn in 1/2 in. on all the outside edges and stitch down with a neat, small in-and-out stitch.

4 Cut two strips of fabric each 10in. x 1in. Fold 1/2 in. in one narrow edge and stitch

down. Fold in the other edges 1/4 in. and tack in place with large stitches. Then line up the strips on the pencil lines and stitch in place with small, neat in-and-out stitches to make a channel. Remove the tacking.

5 Cut two long pieces of yarn for the tails, and stitch to the kite.

6 Cut pieces of fabric 1 1/2 in. x 1/2 in. Use the string to tie these into bows at intervals down the tails.

7 Cut a 20in. length of twine. Stitch the ends through either shoulder and knot in place. This is the bridle.

8 Find the EXACT central point in the bridle and knot it at this point to make a loop. Tie the remaining twine through the loop.

9 Insert the dowels into the channels (trim to fit inside neatly if necessary). Now find a windy spot. Your kite is ready to fly!

★ Cut a piece of thick card to wind your twine around and keep it neat.

★ Make a quick version of this kite using scrap plastic for fabric and straws for dowels. Reinforce the corners with tape before you thread the bridle and tail through them. Tape the straws in place.

Feed the Birds

Make friends with birds by putting out food for them. This bird feeder provides a place where they can perch when they fly in.

Find out about the kinds of birds that live in your area.

Find out what types of foods suit them best, and when is a good time of year to feed them and a good time to let them find their own food.

JOINING WOOD

Here is a simple technique for joining wood with glue and finishing nails. It works perfectly for the projects on this page and page 14.

1 Mark a cross with a pencil where the finishing nails are to go.

2 Place the wood, marked side up, on a surface that won't spoil. A piece of scrap wood is best.

3 Hammer the nails in at each cross so the points just show through on the other side.

4 Now spread wood glue on the other surface to be joined.

5 Press the two pieces together so the finishing nails bite into the glued side. When you have got the position just right, hammer the nails all the way through.

★ It helps if you can clamp the wood firmly while you are hammering. Ask a grown-up for advice on how to do this with the equipment you have on hand.

BIRD FEEDER

This is a great wood-work project for a beginner. The birds don't mind if the wood is rough and unfinished—and they don't mind if the end result is not quite square!

This house is designed to give you practice for making the Noah's ark too! It is based on the same design as the cabin.

metal ruler or woodworker's tape measure

try-square

pencil and paper

saw and workbench

clamp

hand drill with 1/32 in. bit

hammer

1in. paintbrush

1yd piece of pine, about 4in. x 1/2 in.

20in. hardwood strip, about 1/2 in. x 1/2 in.

1yd x 1/4 in. dowel

wood glue

finishing nails, 3/4 in. long

waterproofing stain (choose one that is safe for pets)

6ft rope or thick string

Check with a grown-up before using wood-working tools. Follow the instructions for where and how to use them exactly.

Ask a grown-up to help you select the right waterproofing stain, and to help you use it safely. It is better to use no stain than to use the wrong one, which might be poisonous.

1 Each 4 squares in this diagram represent the width of your wood. Ask a grown-up to help you measure your board accurately and then sketch the shapes on paper, with the correct lengths and widths marked. Then mark the shapes very accurately onto the board. Use the try-square to make sure that all your corners are square.

2 Cut out the pieces with the saw. Label each piece as you cut it on the side that won't show when the feeder is finished.

3 Mark the position of the hole in each side piece and drill it.

4 Mark the sizes of hardwood. Clamp the strip to the workbench so you can safely cut the pieces to the sizes marked. Label them.

5 Mark a point 1/2 in. in from the end of each rafter and drill a hole in it the diameter of the dowel (it will help if you can clamp the wood to the work surface as you drill). Spread glue on the inside of the hole and thread the dowel through, to make a square perch.

6 Center the perch on the base. Spread glue over the part of the rafter that joins the base and press it into position. Use finishing nails to hold it in place.

7 Use the wood-joining technique described here to attach the sides to the base.

8 Use the same technique to nail into place first the narrow roof piece, then the wide roof piece.

9 Apply one or two coats of waterproofing stain, following the instructions for its use very carefully.

10 Thread the rope through the holes and knot as shown. Use the ends of rope to hang the swinging feeder in place.

★ If drilling the rafters is too hard, simply tie the dowel to the rafters after you have completed all the other stages. Or use a thin branch instead of dowel—the birds will happily land on it!

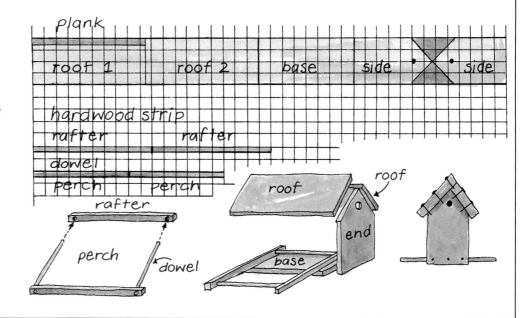

Flood Alert

This Noah's Ark will keep you busy for quite a few wet days! The Bible story about the real Ark tells of the time when there was a great flood. God chose the one good man on the earth, Noah, to build a boat where he, his family and two of every kind of animal would be safe from the rising waters.

You can find out on the next page how to make Noah and the animals.

NOAH'S ARK

The Ark that Noah built had to float well. This one is based on a traditional folk design for a toy to play with on the floor. It is not designed to float in the bath!

You can practice making the cabin part by making the bird feeder, which has almost the same design.

metal ruler or woodworker's tape measure

pencil and paper

saw and workbench

try-square

clamp

plane

sandpaper—medium-fine and extra-fine

hammer

1in. paintbrush

1yd. piece of pine, about 4in. x $^1/_2$in.

5ft. piece of pine, about 2in. x $^1/_2$in. (half the width of the wide piece)

wood glue

finishing nails, $^3/_4$in. long

polyurethane varnish

Check with a grown-up before using woodworking tools. Follow the instructions for where and how to use them exactly.

Ask a grown-up to supervise your using the varnish and to help you clean the brush afterwards. Make sure you work in a well-ventilated place.

1 Each 4 squares in the diagrams for the cabin and the base and sides of the boat represent the width of your wide board. Note that the base and sides of the cabin are $^1/_{16}$ in. narrower than the board (there's a special way to get the board that tiny bit narrower!) Each 2 squares in the diagrams for the boat sides and the ramp represent the width of your narrow board. Ask a grown-up to help you measure your boards accurately and then sketch the shapes onto paper with the lengths and widths correctly marked. Then mark the shapes on the wood.

2 Mark the base and ends of the boat and the back of the cabin on full width pine pieces. Cut these pieces out and label them on the side that won't show. Then cut the roof pieces: cutting along the board can be tricky, so clamp the wood to your workbench and work carefully. Label them.

3 Next, mark a line $^1/_{16}$ in. in from one side of the wide board. You can rule this with a pencil;

however, if you have a marking gauge it will do the job more easily. Plane off this tiny amount. Now you can mark the sides and the floor of the cabin on this slightly narrower board. Cut these pieces out and label them. (The cabin has to be made this tiny bit narrower, so it will slide into the boat.)

4 Now mark the shapes on the narrow board and cut them out. Be sure to label them.

5 Sand all the pieces smooth with medium-fine sandpaper.

6 Assemble the cabin, using the wood-joining technique described on page 13. Attach the back to the base, then put on the sides. Next put on the narrow roof piece, and finally the wide roof piece.

7 Glue and nail the grip to the ramp.

8 Assemble the boat: first glue and nail the ends in place, then the sides.

9 Sand all over the boat and the cabin ark with medium-fine sandpaper one more time. Then dust them clean and apply a coat of polyurethane varnish to all the surfaces except the bit it stands on. Leave to dry, then varnish the base and leave until it is dry.

10 Sand smooth one more time, rubbing lightly with extra-fine sandpaper. Decorate with stencils at this stage if you wish: see the techniques on page 2, and use acrylic paint.

11 Put one more coat of varnish on top.

★ The ramp fits into the front of the ark when it is not needed as a ramp. This helps close up the front.

★ If woodwork seems a bit daunting, try designing and making an ark from cardboard. The ideas here will get you off to a good start.

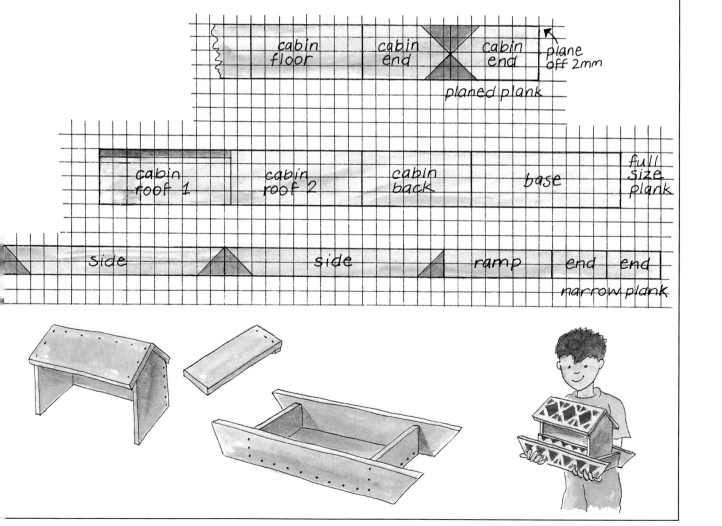

cabin floor   cabin end   cabin end   plane off 2mm

planed plank

cabin roof 1   cabin roof 2   cabin back   base   full size plank

side   side   ramp   end   end

narrow plank

Save the Animals

When the great flood went down, the Bible story goes, God put a rainbow in the sky as a sign that he would never again flood the earth. The animals went out of the ark and had new families. Enjoy finding out about the wonderful designs of animals as you plan the ones for your ark. And think about how you can play your part in caring for the animals of the world.

CUT-OUTS

Traditional folk-animals were cut out of thick wood. Work with a very soft wood, such as balsa or pine, to cut these simple shapes.

coping saw

paper

pencil

clamp to hold the wood as you cut

very fine sandpaper

small paintbrushes

balsa or pine piece, 1/2 in. thick

paint

permanent black marker

1 Draw a simple animal shape the right size for your ark on paper. Work hard to keep the shape as simple as possible.

2 Lay the design on the wood, with the feet flat against a flat edge of the wood. Trace through the design with the pencil to mark the shape on the wood, then go over the shape in pencil directly on the wood.

3 Clamp the wood in place. Cut around the shape slowly and carefully with the coping saw.

4 Sand the edges smooth.

5 Remember to make two of every kind of animal!

6 When you have finished cutting the shapes you want, paint the results as you wish. Use a permanent black marker to add details.

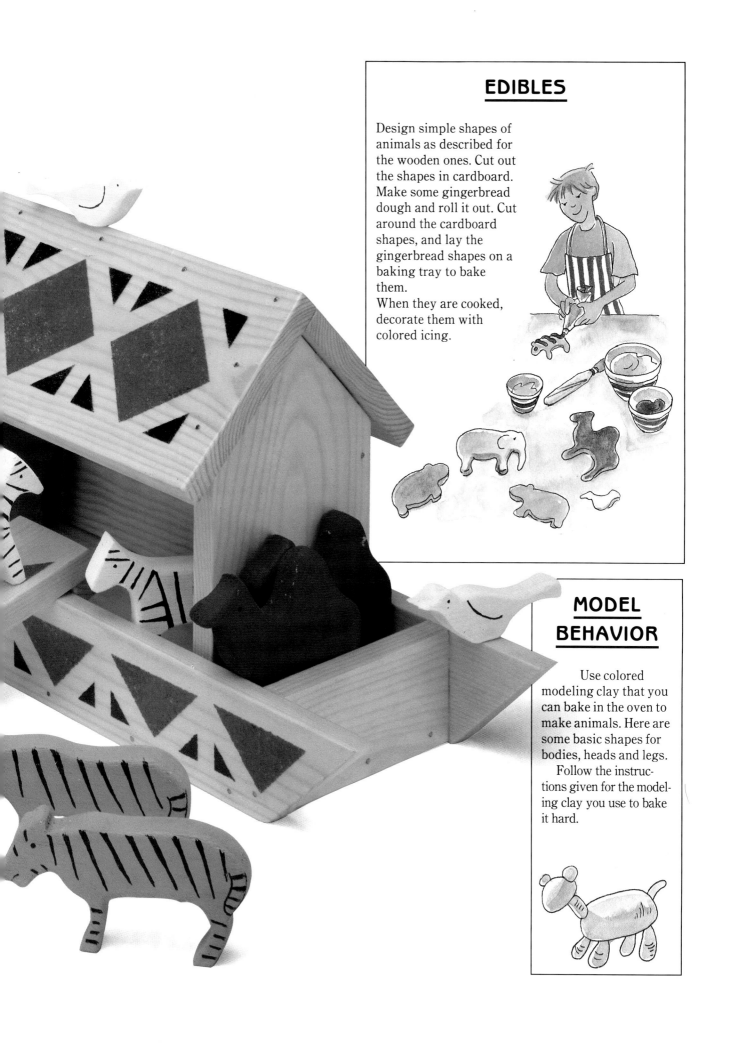

EDIBLES

Design simple shapes of animals as described for the wooden ones. Cut out the shapes in cardboard. Make some gingerbread dough and roll it out. Cut around the cardboard shapes, and lay the gingerbread shapes on a baking tray to bake them.

When they are cooked, decorate them with colored icing.

MODEL BEHAVIOR

Use colored modeling clay that you can bake in the oven to make animals. Here are some basic shapes for bodies, heads and legs.

Follow the instructions given for the modeling clay you use to bake it hard.

Greetings!

Think of the joy you feel at seeing flowers and leaves open up from buds in springtime.

Think of how happy you feel when you open an envelope and find inside a letter from someone who cares about you.

Put those two ideas together to make the most amazing stationery yet from odds and ends of paper! You can use it on all kinds of occasions to make someone happy: staying in touch with old friends, sharing good news and sad news, welcoming newcomers, inviting people over, saying thank-you to people who have remembered you.

LEAF LETTER

scissors

green paper
markers

1 Fold the paper in half and cut out half a leaf shape.

2 Decorate the leaf with markers on one side, and write your letter on the other.

★ Follow the instructions for making leaf prints on page 10, but this time use larger leaves. Print your green paper, and cut around the leaf. Write your letter on the plain side.

BLOOMING BRILLIANT

This flower letter gives you six panels to write on. Try putting one idea—a piece of news, a message, a question—on each panel of the letter. It's easy to write on and easy to read.

pencil and compasses
cutting board or pad of scrap paper
ruler
scissors

colored paper
markers or paints to decorate

1 Protect the table where you are working with a cutting board or scrap paper. Use the ruler and compasses to draw a circle the size you want your flower letter to be.

2 Fold the circle in half. Then fold it into three as shown.

3 Snip a flower petal shape through all thicknesses.

4 Decorate one side of your flower. Write your letter on the other.

BUDDING SUCCESS

If you are hand-delivering your letter, fold an envelope that looks like a bud. (If your letter has to go through the mail, it is better to use a standard, rectangular envelope.)

scissors

paper
tape
glue

1 Cut a square of paper large enough to make an envelope for your letter.

2 Fold and glue as shown.

3 Pop in your flower letter, and perhaps add a folded leaf as well. Fold the flap shut and glue in place.

★ The person who receives a flower and a few leaves can make a pretty decoration from your letter.

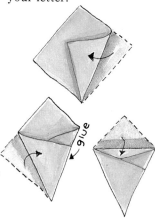

IDEAS GALORE

Look at the ideas for decorating paper on page 2. You can adapt these ideas to decorate all kinds of regular writing paper or to make your own cards.

★ Cut a stencil that provides a border for a particular size of writing paper. Tape the stencil on your pad of paper. Every time you want to write a letter, you can stencil the border in the colors that appeal at the time.

★ Fold thin card in half to make a simple card. Use stenciling to decorate the cards. You can easily make enough for all your family and friends with one or two simple designs.

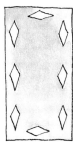

Harvest Fare

Hooray for food! Hooray for the sun and rain that make plants grow so that there are good harvests, with food enough to last all year round.

If there's one thing that's better than simply enjoying food for its own sake, it's sharing a meal with other people. Make people welcome in your home by inviting them over for a meal, using designs to celebrate harvest any day of the year.

A PLACE FOR EVERYONE

Setting a special place for everyone at the table helps make them feel they really belong. Try these British-style wooden placemats, and make plenty of them—enough for everyone you want to welcome.

wood saw and workbench

clamp

ruler and pencil

try-square

medium-fine and extra-fine sandpaper

scrap paper

stencil card

stencil brush

small paintbrush

thin plywood

acrylic paint

clear polyurethane varnish

Check with a grown-up before using woodworking tools. Follow the instructions for where and how to use them exactly.

Ask a grown-up to supervise your using the varnish and to help you clean the brush afterwards. Make sure you work in a well-ventilated place.

1 It's easiest to make square or rectangular mats. Decide how big you want to make them, then use the ruler and pencil to mark that shape on the wood. (The one shown here is 7in. x 7in.)

2 Clamp the wood to the workbench and cut the mats out. Use the medium-fine sandpaper to rub them smooth, especially the cut edges and corners.

3 Dust the mats, then varnish them carefully. You will have to do the top and sides in one session and leave the varnish to dry, and the underside the next time.

4 When the varnish is completely dry all over, rub the mats with extra-fine sandpaper to make them smooth again.

5 Draw around a mat to transfer the shape onto a piece of scrap paper. Work out a stencil design to fit. When you have got it right, copy it onto a stencil card or acetate.

6 Stencil the design onto each mat. Leave to dry.

7 Give the top and sides an extra coat of varnish. Leave to dry very thoroughly.

★ Make larger mats for the center of the table.

RINGS

To make napkin rings, use modeling clay you can bake hard. Roll different colors into thin snakes about 6in. long, braid or twist them together and shape them into rings before baking them.

NEAT NAPKINS

scissors
ruler and pencil
needle

cotton fabric
matching thread
decorative thread

1 Cut your fabric into napkin-sized squares, at least 16in. x 16in. Make sure that each straight edge follows a single thread in the weave of the fabric.

2 Snip off the corners and turn in the edges as shown and stitch down with large stitches you can pull out later.

3 Turn in the edges a second time. First turn each corner down, then fold in the sides neatly. Stitch into place with in-and-out stitches in decorative thread.

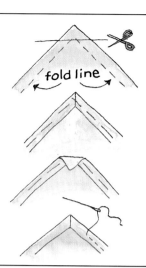

fold line

Happy Christmas

Think of all the things you hope for at Christmas ... the cards and presents, the party invitations and amazing feasts. These things are wonderful in themselves, but all the more so when they show how much people love you.

And you, too, can send cards, give presents, and welcome people to parties. It feels good inside to be able to show people how much you love them.

The heart of the Christmas festival celebrates the birth of a baby called Jesus about 2,000 years ago. He was the person who began the Christian religion, and Christians believe he was God's Son. As a grown man he showed people how to love each other all the time, helping each other in practical ways.

More than that, he came to tell people that God loves them and wants them to turn away from wrongdoing and be his friends.

The Christmas message is a message of love that lasts all year round, for ever.

HEARTS

Hearts are a symbol of love in many countries—just right for Christmas.

scissors
pencil and ruler

paper in several colors
tape
yarn

1 Fold a piece of paper in half, right sides together. Draw a square, about $2^1/_2$ in. x $2^1/_2$ in. on the fold. Top the square with a semi-circle. Cut out this shape.

2 Select a contrasting color of paper, fold it and cut the same shape.

3 Now make two equally spaced cuts down each folded piece so each has three strips. The cuts should be as high as the square.

4 Fold the pieces right side out and weave them together. Take the lowest strip from the piece in your right hand and weave it into the piece in your left hand: into the first strip, around the next, and into the third.

5 Take the middle strip from the piece in your right hand and weave it into the left around the first strip, into the next, and around the third.

6 Take the final strip from the piece in your right hand and weave it into the left piece: into the first strip, around the next, and into the third. If this seems too hard, you may need to undo the basket, make all the cuts a little longer, and try again. You'll soon have the knack of it.

7 Open up your basket. Use tape to attach a paper or a yarn handle. Now you are ready to add the small gift and hang the basket on the Christmas tree.

★ Have extra hearts with tiny treats inside for any surprise visitors, old or young.

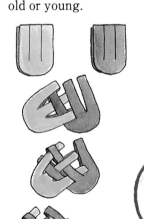

MAKE-YOUR-OWN PARTY

Hide a party in the heart baskets you make for your Christmas tree. Spend some time before Christmas thinking of games to play with the people you'll be with. Write each on a slip of paper and put it in the heart. When you need something to do, ask someone to select a heart, and play the game that's suggested inside.

★ Catch!
Make tiny egg-shaped cups by molding papier mâché around egg shells or tiny plastic pots. Follow the directions for the papier mâché bowl on page 19—only the bowl is MUCH smaller!

Now make colored pompoms (page 8) and tie them with a long piece of yarn so you have one long end. Thread this on a needle and stitch it to the side of the cup.

Each player holds their cup, leaving the pompom dangling. Then they flick the cup and try to catch the pompom in it. Who is the best at catching it? Can you teach *everyone* the knack of catching it?

★ Memory Game
Make sure you have a set of Leaf-Lookalikes ready for Christmastime and play the memory game described on page 10.

★ Merry Mice
The Mighty Mice described on page 11 love Christmas merriment. Play the Three Around game ... or have a juggling contest.

★ Mouse Hole
Decorate a strong cardboard box (see the ideas on page 1) or find a clean trash can. See who can toss the Mighty Mice into it most accurately. Younger people may need to stand closer than grown-ups.

★ Animal Hunt
Hide your Noah's Ark animals (page 15) around the house and get people to search for them. Who can find the most? Who finds the most pairs? If this game is popular, give other people the chance to hide the animals.

★ Three-in-a-Row
Draw simple Three-in-a-Row boards (see page 10) on card or paper and cut card playing pieces for each (or find buttons to use as playing pieces). Let everyone play with different people taking turns.

★ Feely Game
Make a large bag (page 5) and fill it with all kinds of treasures: nuts, shells, spools of thread, tiny jars, wrapped candy and so on. Everyone takes a turn to put their hand in and feel for an object. If they can say what it is, they pull it out. Who can guess the best? Who has the funniest ideas?

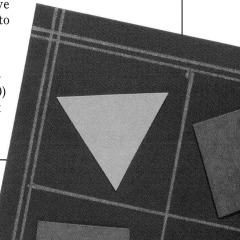

Easter Joys

Traditional Easter decorations are all about new life: about baby birds and animals, about buds opening on bare branches, and flowers opening fantastic petals in glorious colors.

At this time Christians remember something even more amazing. About 2,000 years ago, Jesus, the founder of Christianity, was put to death. Three days later, his friends saw him alive again. He had beaten death, and he promised his followers that anyone who believed in him would have new life now and always.

That new life would be full of hope and happiness, as different from the old life as spring is different from winter.

The Easter message is a message of new life.

BEAUTIFUL BOWL

You can't make an egg that hatches, and you can't make a plant that grows. Try the next best thing, with a beautiful pot that will hold growing plants.

You make them just like the gift eggs opposite, except that you only cover each balloon two-thirds of the way up.

Remember to put extra papier mâché over the edges and on the inside.

Make sure your plant stands inside a waterproof plastic pot inside the bowl, to protect the papier mâché.

the same materials as for egg boxes opposite

★ It is best to lift the plant pots out of the bowl when you water them.

★ Try growing plants from seeds or bulbs. Ask a grown-up to help you plan ahead, so you can have plants and planters ready to give as Easter gifts.

GIFT EGGS

Make an egg-shaped papier mâché box in which to give someone a special Easter gift. You may decide to hide your gift eggs and ask family and friends to hunt for them.

balloons

bowl and old spoon

plate

bucket

wire rack

scissors

paintbrushes

old newspaper

scrap paper that is plain on one side

wallpaper paste

thin card

tape

paint

varnish

1 Blow up the balloon to the size you want your box to be and tie it shut.

2 Tear the newspaper and paper into squares, perhaps 6in. x 6in. (any easy-to-handle size will do). Keep them in separate piles.

3 Mix the wallpaper paste with water in the bowl, following the instructions that come with it. It will be very thick.

4 Fill the bucket with water and dip a piece of newspaper in it. Then lay it on the plate, and brush it all over on both sides with wallpaper paste.

5 Tear off small bits of pasted paper and cover the balloon with them, overlapping each piece carefully. You will need to use several squares of paper for each layer. Leave on a wire rack to dry overnight.

6 Now cover the balloon with a layer of plain paper. (Having two sorts of paper helps you see where you have added strips!) Again, let it dry.

7 Add another layer of newspaper, and in a final session another layer of plain paper. Leave the balloon to dry again, this time pressing it a little so that it makes a flat place where it can 'sit' without rolling.

8 When you are sure the paper is dry, snip the balloon to let the air out. Draw a line around halfway as shown, and carefully cut along that line to make two halves.

9 Use some of the strips of plain paper in the paste to wrap over the cut edges, to line the inside, and to fill in the opening where the balloon neck used to be. Leave to dry.

10 Paint the egg one color inside and another color outside. Add painted patterns if you wish.

11 When the paint is dry, varnish it if you wish, for extra shine.

12 Cut 2 strips of thin card each 1in. wide and long enough to fit down a side of the edge of one half. Tape them in place. These are the flanges that will hold the lid in place—your egg box is ready!

★ To make sure the lid stays in place, tie it on with a ribbon and knot it into a bow.

Gifts for Everyone

Think of all the occasions for giving gifts: Christmas and Easter, birthdays, special days for moms and dads, times when people are sad or unwell and need something to cheer them.

Giving gifts is a way of showing that you care. Making gifts is even more special.

It shows you have spent time looking for ideas in the world around you, and that you want to share what you have found with the other person.

It shows that you think it's worth spending time making something to please them.

The fact that the result is the only one of its kind can help show just how special your relationship with them is.

IN THE BAG

It's worth spending a bit of time getting the trick of folding a bag like this. Once you can do it easily, you can turn all kinds of paper into elegant wrappings for oddly-shaped gifts.

scissors
ruler

wrapping paper
tape

1 Follow these folding and taping instructions. Do each stage neatly—it will make the next one much easier.

2 Fold the paper like this and tape.

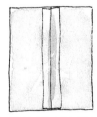

3 Snip off the bottom corners.

4 Fold up the bottom edge and tape.

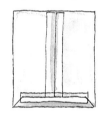

5 Fold in the sides, the same amount each side. Crease and uncrease. Then fold up the lower edge the same amount, and then make a second fold up accordion fashion.

first fold up

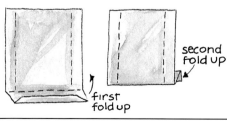

second fold up

6 Pleat the sides inwards and fold out the 'ears' on the bottom.

7 Fold up the base as shown and tape the ears down. This is the tricky bit, but worth the hassle the first time you try!

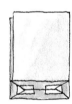

★ Use a thick needle to thread yarn or ribbon through the top to fasten the bag shut.

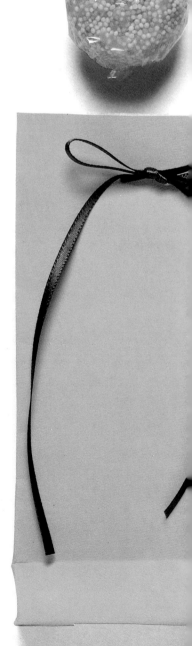

SIMPLE SACHET

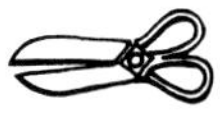

large plate
pencil and ruler
empty ball pen

scissors
thin card
tape

1 Fold and tape the card as shown.

2 Line the ruler up at each end and make a tiny pencil mark at the folded edge.

3 Now draw around a plate to mark curved shapes as shown.

4 Score a cut with an old pen or (very carefully) with a craft knife along the inner curves. Do this on both sides.

5 Cut out around the outer curves.

6 Fold the curves in so they overlap each other. Tape shut if you wish.

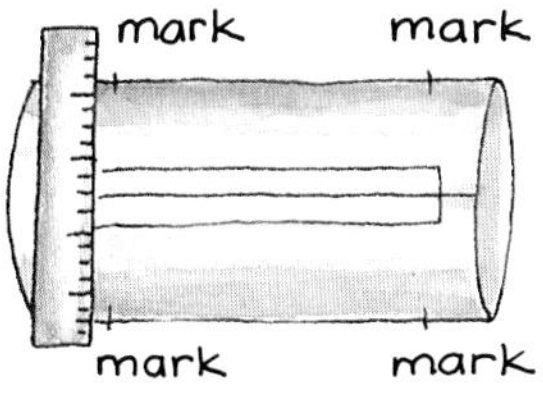

mark   mark

mark   mark

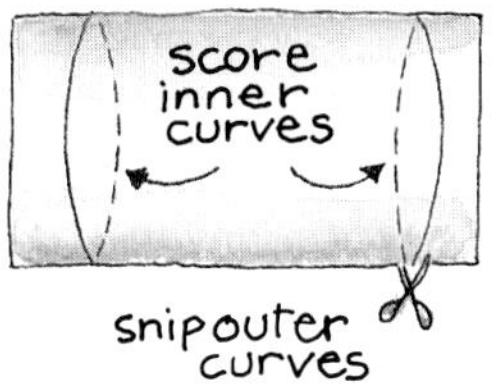

score
inner
curves

snip outer
curves

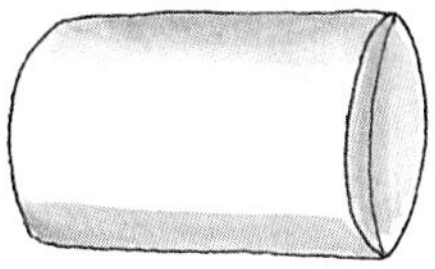

PROJECTS

TIPS AND TECHNIQUES
Basic sewing stitches

Begin your sewing with a knot. Wind a loop of thread around the first finger of your right hand. Roll it off with your right thumb, then pinch the roll between your thumb and forefinger and pull the loop tight.

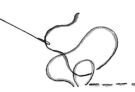

Tie off the end by taking a small backstitch. Before pulling it tight, loop the thread like this. Then pull to make a tight knot.

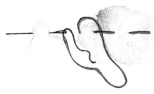

Tacking stitches are for holding work together while you do the real stitches. They are simply big in-and-out stitches. Make them about $1/2$ in. long, so they are quick to work and easy to pull out.

In-and-out stitches can be between $1/8$ in. and $1/4$ in. long. Decide on what looks right for the project, and then try to keep them all the same.

Backstitch is a strong stitch for seams. Make each stitch about $1/8$ in. long.

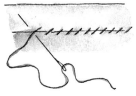

Hemming is a small slanting stitch. Keep it small and even. Check that the stitch that shows on the other side is small and neat.

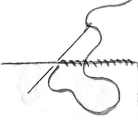

Over-and-over stitch consists of small stitches close together like this:

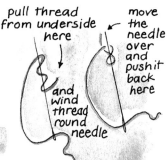

pull thread from underside here

move the needle over and push it back here

and wind thread round needle

Knot stitch is worked like this. Practice with a spare scrap of fabric and thread to get the hang of it.

Scissors, paper and glue

Always protect work surfaces when doing crafts.

Protect yourself too!

Choose craft scissors with rounded ends.
If you use a craft knife, be sure to choose a safety knife with a blade that can be locked with just a tiny bit of cutting edge.

Always cut onto a cutting mat, or a thick pad of scrap paper.

Always wear an apron to protect yourself from glue and paint.

Some glues and paints give off fumes. Always work in a well-ventilated place, perhaps close to an open window.